Chase and Sanborn

Presented with Compliments of Chase and Sanborn

Importers of and Wholesale Dealers in Teas and Coffees

Chase and Sanborn

Presented with Compliments of Chase and Sanborn
Importers of and Wholesale Dealers in Teas and Coffees

ISBN/EAN: 9783337046897

Printed in Europe, USA, Canada, Australia, Japan

Cover: Foto ©Andreas Hilbeck / pixelio.de

More available books at **www.hansebooks.com**

PRESENTED

WITH COMPLIMENTS

OF

CHASE & SANBORN,

Importers of and Wholesale Dealers in

TEAS & COFFEES,

Nos. 87 BROAD AND 8 HAMILTON STREETS,

BOSTON, MASS., U. S. A.

SOLE IMPORTERS AND DISTRIBUTERS OF

STANDARD JAVA.

WE DEDICATE

THIS LITTLE PAMPHLET, INSIGNIFICANT AS IT IS, TO THE

RETAIL GROCERS OF NEW ENGLAND,

GRATEFULLY REMEMBERING,

THAT THROUGH THEIR SUPPORT, WE HAVE BEEN ENABLED TO BUILD UP

A LARGE AND

CONSTANTLY INCREASING BUSINESS IN OUR SPECIALTIES

TEAS AND COFFEES.

INTRODUCTORY.

We have launched a small craft and trust it will find a snug harbor in every Retail Grocer's establishment in New England.

Its cargo consists of facts and information which we have gathered from our experience as a Coffee house and also from Importers, who have spent their entire lives in the business. We are practical business men, who desire to furnish what information we can, in a plain matter of fact manner, believing it is for our mutual interests, that you should be informed in regard to a staple article which enters so largely into your daily sales.

In disclosing trade secrets and uncovering prevailing frauds, we have not been actuated by an aggressive spirit, but believe it is time that ignorance and its partner humbug, should retire and make way for intelligence and progress.

Should you be able to glean any fresh .information from this volume, that would enable you to purchase and place before the consumer a better cup of coffee, then shall we feel that our time, labor and expense have been amply repaid.

THE PROPERTIES OF COFFEE.

COFFEE, as a beverage, is too well known to require an extended notice. We are a nation of coffee-drinkers, consuming over one third of the entire production of the world. You find it in the abode of the poor as well as the rich; no breakfast table is considered complete without it, and how often you hear the very significant remark, "I can make my breakfast off a cup of coffee."

Coffee contains valuable medicinal properties; among others, that of being anti-soporific, and hence useful in cases of narcotic poisoning. Coffee has frequently been found the best form of stimulant for administration to persons rescued from starvation, or perishing by cold; and this is the more noteworthy, as ardent spirits given under the same conditions often prove fatal.

Captain Parry, when on his Arctic expedition, put his starboard watch on coffee, and the port watch on rum; and the result was that, in the course of time, the coffee watch was found to possess a vigor of health entirely wanting in the other. As late as 1835, during a terrible epidemic, the physicians of New York signed a public manifesto urging the public to abstain from beer and intoxicating liquors, and drink pure coffee, in order to keep the system healthy, and render it less liable to disease. From all quarters testimony without limit might be accumulated to the same effect.

7

As a disinfecting agent, roasted coffee is invaluable ; it is useful to purify any place having an offensive smell or foul air. The coffee beans should be roasted in the vicinity of the room to be fumigated, and when brown and while hot, placed in the centre. By the time the coffee is cooled, the room will be rendered thoroughly pure and sweet.

HISTORY OF COFFEE.

LTHOUGH we are all familiar with coffee as a beverage, yet, comparatively few of us know the history of its origin, where it was first grown, when introduced, how cultivated and cured.

Accounts differ as to when, where, and by whom coffee was first introduced to civilization. An eastern legend ascribes the discovery of the berry to a dervish who, in the year 1285, being driven out of Mocha, was induced in the extremity of hunger to roast the berries which grew near his hiding place. He ate them, and steeping the roasted berries in water to quench his thirst, discovered their agreeable qualities. But a more authentic account states that it was introduced into Arabia from Southern Abyssinia (where it is indigenous) by a Mohammedan high priest, about the year 1500. We are indebted to the Persians for the discovery of the roasting process, and as the merits of coffee as a beverage would have remained unknown without that, some authorities allow them the credit of being the first introducers. It continued its career through Syria, and in the year 1554, we learn it became the favorite drink at Constantinople, and the oriental coffee houses were thronged night and day. The lower classes actually begged money for coffee, and it is stated that the refusing to supply a wife with coffee was admitted in law as a valid cause for divorce. Europeans are indebted to the Dutch for their first acquaintance with the coffee plant. This was brought

9

about in the following manner : some berries, which had in the first place been procured, were carried to the island of Java and there planted. A specimen plant was sent home to Amsterdam in 1690, by Gov. Wilson. This plant bore fruit, from which many young trees were propagated, and from this original, most of the gardens of Europe and the East Indies are supposed to have been furnished.

In 1714 a plant was presented by the magistrates of Amsterdam to the French King, Louis XIV. This plant was carefully nursed, and from this source plants were forwarded some years later to the French West India Islands, and from these all the coffee now found in the Western Hemisphere derives its origin.

The Parisians immediately adopted the drink, and it became the fashionable beverage of Paris. It could only be indulged in by the wealthy few, as the price was exorbitant. It is stated that a sum equivalent to $15,000 per year was expended for supplying the daughters of Louis XV with the beverage. The English owe to Mr. Edwards a Turkey merchant, their knowledge of coffee. This gentleman, about the year 1650, brought to England, a Greek youth, who used to prepare the drink for his master ; the latter, however, finding that the novelty began to attract too many visitors to his house, gave the boy his liberty, and enabled him to open a coffee-house on his own account.

At first it met with violent opposition ; it was denounced as "hell drink," "hell poison," etc. A heavy tax was imposed upon it by the legislature, but, notwithstanding all opposition, the beverage constantly gained ground, and coffee-houses were as plentiful in London as at Constantinople.

Across the water the custom jumped, and the infant United States commenced to nourish its strength from the coffee-pot, and in no place in the world, probably, are the influences more healthful, the effects more happily displayed than in this country, especially at the " Old French

Market," in New Orleans. The coffee-vendors are distributed throughout the market place and streets, and are kept as busy as bees supplying cups of coffee to the European, Creole, New Englander, Westerner, who, standing side by side in the open street, forget caste, and sip the nectar. The coffee-houses of New York are intimately associated with the history of the city. Here were gathered the leading literary, professional and mercantile men, who discussed the leading topics of the day while sipping their cups of coffee.

But the coffee-house is a thing of the past. The more pretentious club house has taken its place, and the lovers of coffee are forced to the restaurant for their favorite drink.

THE PLANT & ITS CULTIVATION.

AVING in the last chapter traced the history of coffee from the year 1500 up to the present date, we shall now endeavor to describe the nature of the plant and the method of cultivation.

The coffee plant is more the nature of a shrub, growing to the height of 12 to 15 feet in its wild state, but under cultivation, is kept down to six or eight feet by careful pruning and cutting, which increases the quality and quantity of its product, and lessens the labor of picking the berries. The tree grows erect, with a single stem opening out at the upper part into long, drooping branches, which seldom grow to any great thickness. Its leaves in general appearance, resemble those of the common laurel, although not so hard or dry, being oval and sharp-pointed ; from the angle of the leaf stalk, small groups of white flowers appear, numbering from four to twelve in a group ; they very much resemble a jessamine blossom in scent and form, being funnel-shaped and very fragrant. The flowering of the plant frequently occurs in a single night, and lasts but a few days, although in some countries the plant flowers and bears fruit the entire year. The fruit, or berries which succeed the blossom, resemble a cherry in size, are at first dark green, but soon change their hue—first to yellow, then to red, until finally they become a dark crimson. When this stage is reached they are ripe and ready to be gathered. The external part of the fruit, under the skin, is a pulpy mass, somewhat glutinous in character, which envelopes two oval seeds, these being convex on one side and flat on the other, lie with the flat sides in contact face to face, separated by a thin parchment or skin, and are the coffee beans of commerce.

It frequently happens that only one seed forms : this seed, in process of growth, pushes itself against the dividing membrane, and encountering no opposing growth, naturally rounds itself, and produces a small round bean, known as the male-berry, or pea-berry.

In selecting a spot to locate a coffee plantation, the same general rules are observed throughout the coffee-growing districts of the world, viz : equable climate and a rich virgin soil, where the forest has been growing thick and heavy. Decayed trees and decomposed leaves accumulating for centuries, form a thick mould, which the coffee plant flourishes the best on. The planter selects moderately gentle slopes or hillside, protected from wind, which is sure death to the plants, with running streams for irrigating purposes, as a constant even moisture is necessary for the full development of the plant. Land being selected, his next move is to secure his plants. These are sometimes obtained by taking root shoots from the old fields, care being taken to select from a healthy plant, and set out at once into prepared ground. But in the cultivation of coffee the same relative improvements have been made that exist in other industries, and the modern method is to select young and thriving plants from the nurseries. These are set out in holes in order to secure a constant supply of water, and are arranged in rows from eight to ten feet apart. By pursuing this more recent method, the planter secures not only a healthier lot of trees but obtains a crop about a year in advance. At the end of three years, the plants commence bearing a small crop, but do not fully mature in less than six years, when the crops are usually very large, a single tree frequently bearing from three to four lbs. of berries. The limit of productiveness for a coffee plant is about thirty years, after that age if any fruit forms it is almost worthless. The plantations require constant care, weeds must be removed, the trees kept moist by watering, either naturally or artificially. (By glancing at colored engraving in front of book you will be able to get a perfect idea of the leaves, flowers and fruit of a coffee plant.)

HARVESTING AND CURING.

E now come to the harvesting of the berries, and as noted in our last chapter, the fruit is ready for picking when it assumes a dark crimson color. The time of picking varies according to the temperature of the producing countries. The crop begins to ripen in Brazil in May and continues until November. In Java, picking commences about the first of January, lasting three or four months. The Ceylon crop is gathered from April to July. The crop rarely ripens all at once, except on very young trees, and in order to insure the coffee arriving at perfection and so earning a high reputation in the market, the careful planter does not pick the berries until fully ripe. To insure this, three pickings are usually considered necessary, in order to gather the berries as they ripen. The first and third are usually light ones, the bulk of the crop being obtained on the second gathering. The labor of picking is usually performed by women and children, who are furnished with two bags, a large and small one, the former being sufficiently large to tie up when containing an imperial bushel and a half. The smaller one is worn round the waist of the picker to receive the berries as they are gathered from the tree. In the height of the crop season, the pickers can gather in a day about three bushels apiece, for which, in Ceylon, they are paid four pence a bushel, and about the same ratio of payment holds good, throughout the coffee growing districts. The next process is to remove the pulp surrounding the seeds, and for this, different methods are used. The old system was, after gathering, to spread the crop out on high level terraces, exposed to the sun's rays, then when thoroughly dried, heavy rollers were passed and repassed over the berries until the outer pulp was thoroughly cracked. Great improvements have been made on the old method by the introduction of machinery, and we will give a description of the modes employed in Brazil, which to-day is far ahead of all other countries in the preparation of coffee. As pursued there, the processes of preparation are first, the removal of the outer pulp by maceration in water ; second, the drying of the seeds with their coverings ; third, the removal of the several coverings after they are dry. To these three processes is sometimes added a fourth, by which the seeds are assorted according to their sizes and forms. Above the mills there is a cement lined trough, through which runs a strong stream of water. Through a funnel shaped opening, the coffee berries are thrown into the stream which carries them down with it to a large vat, a pipe draws off the heavier berries to the pulping machine, while the lighter ones (which are almost valueless) are floated on the surface water to another pipe. The pulping machine is simply a revolving iron cylinder, set with teeth and covered on one side by a curved sheet of metal, against which it crowds as it turns. It is in fact, a nutmeg grater on a large scale. The berries carried to the cylinder by the stream of water, are crushed between it and the cover, and the pulp is thus loosened. Passing from this to a vat beyond, the water is kept in constant motion by a rapidly revolving wheel; by this means, the pulp is thoroughly washed off and carried away with the water, while the heavier seeds sink to the bottom ; thence they are carried to a strainer, which drains off the water and leaves the seeds ready for the next stage. The seeds are still enclosed together in the outer and inner shell. The next process is that of drying and is effected in two different ways. The old way is to spread the seeds out and dry in the sun, which consumes about sixty days ; during that time the seeds must be raked over and turned during the day and gathered in piles and covered at night or before it rains. The new system is drying by steam. In a long, low building will be found rows of zinc covered tables, with steam pipes running beneath them upon which the seeds are placed. The berries are constantly stirred with wooden rakes and removed when dry. The steam process must supplant the old system entirely, as by it the coffee is dried thoroughly in a few hours, and the product is much improved in quality. The coffee grains are still enclosed in their inner and outer parchment like shells, now dry and brittle. The removal of these is effected by machines, which resemble a threshing and fanning machine, which by a constant grinding and pounding produce nice clean coffee beans. The coffee now passes to the separator, which is composed of a pair of revolving cylinders pierced with holes of different sizes and shapes. The beans being placed in the cylinders, fall through these holes and are sorted by them into large and small, flat and round grains, which pass into different bins, finally picked over by hand and then consigned to sacks for transportation to the shipping port. After reaching which, the coffee is packed in bags or mats and offered for sale.

VARIETIES OF COFFEES.

THE range of coffee culture extends over almost the whole of the tropical belt of the globe, flourishing best on highlands ranging from 1,500 to 5,000 feet, and between the 5th and 15th degree of latitude, north and south of the equator. Indigenous varieties of the plant are found growing in Brazil, Peru, Central America, Java and Sumatra, Ceylon, So. India, Africa, (including Abyssinia, Natal, Gold Coast, Liberia,) Arabia, Manilla, the Mauritius, in the West India Islands and islands of the Pacific. But Brazil in the Western Hemisphere, Java, Sumatra, Ceylon and India in the Eastern Hemisphere, constitute at this time the great centre for coffee production.

 Coffee is divided commercially into two classes, strong and mild. Strong coffee includes Rio and Santos, but more particularly Rio. East India coffee embraces all coffee raised east of the Cape of Good Hope, and with the exception of Mocha is principally raised on islands. They are Javas, Ceylons, Malabars, and Madagascars.

The strong coffees, Rio and Santos, are a product of Brazil, a country, which, although in its infancy, is to-day supplying over one half of the entire coffee crop of the world. The coffee of Brazil varies greatly in size and color. Most of the Rio received here is a small sized bean, varying in color from a light to a dark green, with some of a yellow hue known as Golden Rio. In flavor it is peculiarly distinct from all other coffee grown, being very

18

rank and strong. It is shipped from the port of Rio Janeiro principally. The principal ports of entry in the United States, are New York, Baltimore and New Orleans. The coffee was formerly controlled by a few, rich importers through bankers, and sold to jobbers, who re-sold to the wholesale grocers throughout the United States. But the establishing of a line of fast steamers has completely revolutionized the importation. The time now occupied in a passage averages only about 30 days and it is in the power of any man, with funds sufficient to purchase an exchange draft, to import small quantities. The Eastern coffee jobbers now receive Rio direct and sell or consign to our Western States, although some of the larger western jobbers are themselves importing direct. The West and South are the great consumers of Rio. The theory advanced for this, is, that the waters of those sections are so completely filled with lime, that the fine properties so highly prized in the mild coffees in the East are destroyed or killed in the making.

Santos coffee is produced in the southern districts of the Brazilian Empire, and possesses in a mild degree all the characteristics of Rio ; it is shipped in the same vessels with Rio coffee, and its sale is conducted in the same manner. The total yearly production of Brazil amounts to a trifle over 550,000,000 lbs., or as we previously said, over one half of the entire coffee crop of the world. Of this the United States absorbs the largest portion of the Rio export, while Europe takes about 85 per cent. of the Santos.

Mild coffees embrace all coffees except Rio and Santos. Some of them are very rank and of positive flavor ; they are sold separately or are mixed and combined in such a manner as to lose their individuality. The most prominent of all mild coffees is Java ; this is raised on the islands of Java and Sumatra and ranks first in the estimation of the coffee drinking public of the United States.

Java coffee is classified as follows: Fancy Marks, Interiors, Preangers, Samarangs, Malangs, Kadoes, Passoeroeangs, Sumatras and Singapores.

Fancy Marks include Mandehling, Ayer-Bangies, Ankola. These are the names of the districts from which the coffees derive their names. They are valued high, commercially, owing to the comparatively small amount raised, composing only about 10 or 15 per cent. of the entire export of Javas. The bean is large and stylish, drinks rich and strong, but lacks the finer qualities of private plantation Javas, which we shall refer to later.

Interiors, so called, from being raised in the interior of the island of Sumatra, are better known in this country as Padang Java, deriving that name from the port of shipment, which is Padang. They comprise the larger part of the Java coffee sold in this country, and for years have been considered a very superior coffee. They are not so stylish as Fancy Marks ; drink rich and strong, and possess a characteristic flavor of their own.

Preanger, raised on the island of Java, is somewhat different from Padang, both in style and drink, being a smaller bean and ranker, or stronger in the cup. The standard of excellence is not being kept up and it is not so highly prized as formerly. At one time it outranked interior Padang.

Samarangs, Malangs, Kadoes, Passoeroeangs, can be described under one head, closely resembling each other in one leading characteristic, namely : Inferiority, and sell for about 20 per cent. less than Interior Padangs. Although grown on the island they are a disgrace to the place of their nativity. The mild coffees of So. America actually excel them in style and drinking qualities, and were it not for the all-powerful name of Java, which they bear, they would not be recognized as even approaching fineness.

They are sold largely in the Eastern States, paying a large profit· to wholesale dealers, and at the same time easing their consciences, by allowing them to sell a straight Java coffee and literally doing so, but in no particular, contributing a coffee that will suit the consumer.

Sumatra coffee is raised on the island of Sumatra, and is known commercially as Free Java, from the fact that the Dutch Government have no control over the growth or sale of it. It is a large, irregular bean and drinks inferior. Little care being taken in the cultivation and curing ; a large proportion of it arrives here in a condition known as ground stained, which we shall refer to later.

Singapore Java embraces coffee raised adjacent to and shipped from Singapore, but the same grade is also shipped from Macassai and Bonthyne. Each of them has a peculiar taste, which renders it very disagreeable, although we have been assured by English coffee importers, that it is the finest coffee raised, yet no greater insult can be offered to an intelligent coffee dealer in this country than to ask him to buy Singapore coffee. This coffee, years ago, was very freely imported into this country and largely sold west ; but as its character became known the consumption as Singapore Java ceased. In fact, although large quantities are imported into this country, it is a common remark, that there never is a lb. sold. The plain English of it is, that it is recolored in New York, (chemically), and sold as Padang. Lately there has been imported into the United States what is called plantation coffee, that is, coffee raised from fine selected seed on large private estates on the Island of Java, such estates being under the best agricultural conditions, with unlimited capital and intelligent manipulation, produce a coffee which in the cup makes a drink that in our opinion is the finest ever produced ; under the above conditions some of these plantations have acquired a reputation that has reached all over the world, and recently some of the more enterprising coffee dealers have imported these coffees largely. They are sold on contract or tenders, that is, as soon as the quality and quantity of his crop can be estimated, the planter issues tenders and solicits bids ; if, when the bids are opened, the price is below his views, then he claims the right to reject them and hold his goods. But such is the reputation of these plantations, and the known high quality of their products that there is great competition and the crop sells high.

The sale of Padang Java is conducted on a different basis from any other coffee. It is advertised and sold under the auspices of the Dutch government in quarterly sales, occurring in the months of March, June, September and December. It is put up at auction, in one hundred picul lots, (a Picul is 133⅓ lbs.) and no buyer can purchase more than this quantity at one bidding. The price varies at each sale, and no party buying in any considerable quantity on unlimited orders, can tell what his coffee will average to cost until the whole sale is ended. The price of each quarterly sale varies with the amount advertised, and the orders received by the agents to buy.

Interior Padang Java is raised on government or wild land. The native is furnished with the seed by the Government, which insists that he shall keep in good bearing order not less than 650 trees, and his crop, if up to the required standard, is taken by the government at a certain fixed price. After being accepted it is stored in godowns or warehouses which are built open at the sides, consequently the hot winds have free access to it and it matures or ripens in proportion to the length of time it remains in store. A proportion of the Fancy Marks are sold in same manner.

Java coffee, regardless of quality, is always shipped in grass mats, varying in weight, from 60 to 80 lbs. each. Upon the mats are plain marks which usually indicate the importer, and the district where the contents were grown. Viz : the mark, $\frac{C \& S}{I}$ would denote that Chase & Sanborn were the importers, and the contents were Interior Javas ;

the letters K—S—P—M underneath would respectively signify Kadoe, Samarang, Passoeroeang, Malang.

Java coffee possesses one feature peculiar to no other coffee, namely, that of turning very decidedly brown or yellow, but more especially brown.

Interior and fancy Padangs possess this peculiarity more than other varieties. If this color were a sure indication of age, we should freely concur with the views of the trade generally, that a brown Java possessed finer drinking qualities than a pale. While we do believe that age does improve its drinking qualities, we as firmly believe that the color (if natural) in no particular adds to or detracts from its value in the cup. And we have given this subject careful practical attention and investigation.

What produces the brown color? How it is obtained? is to-day what it has been from the time the first pound was imported, a " huge mystery."

The general theory is that it is caused by steaming or sweating in the hold of the vessel while on the passage. But why coffee grown on the same land, picked and cured at the same time, and shipped on the same vessel, should, on arrival at New York, be found to vary in color from very pale to a decided brown is a conundrum which refuses to be solved satisfactorily. Various experiments have been tried. At one time pepper packed in the hold with the coffee was supposed to produce the coveted result. A cargo of coffee was shipped under the above conditions and the outturn was a beautiful brown cargo. The same vessel brought another shipment later, the same identical conditions being carefully observed, and on removing the hatches what was the owners chagrin to find the mystery still a mystery; his coffee was as pale as when loaded.

Practically, the demand for a brown Java is an American caprice which has enhanced its commercial value two to three cents per lb. and this caprice is also directly responsible for the immense quantity of imitation brown Java, which is at present flooding the market.

Wholesale dealers demand brown Java and reject pale, what is the result? Yankee ingenuity steps in and supplies the demand by converting (by the aid of poisonous chemicals), large bean, South American mild coffees and Singapore into brown Padang Java, which only experts can detect, as far as style is concerned. In New York City, tons of such coffee are produced daily. And this condition of affairs will exist just as long as it is the exception rather than the rule, for wholesale dealers to buy coffee on style and color and neglect through carelessness (but oftener ignorance), to roast and test samples in the cups after the manner of testing teas. To sum up our argument, we would say that while we do not claim that pale Java is better than brown, we do insist that it is in every particular its equal in cup value and less liable to manipulations in this country. And should you continue demanding Old Brown Java, we believe the chances are that 50 per cent. of your purchases will consist of imitations, and for the balance, if genuine, you will pay 3 to 5 cents per lb. for color, without, in any particular, improving its quality. Make drinking qualities your standard for determining excellence, and do not continue to be deceived by color, style, or trade names, such as, "Old Government Java." This term arises from the fact that the Dutch Government formerly held considerable quantities for a long time before selling it, and this was usually of very good quality. Old Government Java soon became a trade term denoting highest quality. Of late years this term has been used indiscriminately to designate all Javas of whatever quality and ceased to possess any real significance as to extra merit.

Mocha, the aristocratic coffee of the world, is grown in Arabia. It is found on both sides of the Red Sea, that on the north side coming from Hodgeda and commonly called "genuine Arabian Mocha," is raised in very hot and dry localities. The bean is very small and irregular in appearance, drinks rank, acrid and peculiar, and when roasted is one of the most unsightly coffees grown—invariably quakery—owing to the intense heat prevalent where the coffee grows. This is transported to Aden, (the shipping port), on the backs of camels. Here it is shelled and matted for shipment. The United States are the principal consumers of this grade. That which comes from the south, from the Berbia district, has quite a large bean, drinks well, and is prized very highly. Quite lately it has been shipped to the United States and its intrinsic merit as it becomes known, will eventually make it very desirable. Probably no one kind of coffee coming to the United States is so generally adulterated or counterfeited. Vast quantities of Malabar and small bean Ceylons are shipped to Alexandria, then matted and exported as genuine Mocha.

The Mocha coffee trade of Aden is principally controlled by Armenians or Parsee Hindoos, although there are two or three German and French houses engaged in the trade, but these ship principally to France and the Continent. For a great many years the importation of Mocha coffee was in the hands of the now venerable John Bertram, Esq., of Salem, Massachusetts, and since his retirement, by Messrs. Arnold, Hines & Co., of New York, and George Ropes, Esq. of Boston, and although there may be at times genuine Mocha coffee imported by others into this country, yet so successfully and honorably have these concerns above named imported these goods, that to buy their brands seems to be the public's only guarantee of obtaining the true article. It was not our intention to advertise any man's goods in preference to another, but as this is an article which commands the highest price of any coffee on the list, we deem it our privilege to put the trade on the right track in buying the same, more especially as the talent for adulteration and imitation is being so rapidly developed. For a long time it was supposed that the strong, unique packages such as enclose Mocha coffee, could not be tampered with or opened and closed again successfully, but by steaming the materials or bagging, the large withes by which it is sewed are carefully drawn out, the contents changed or adulterated, and the package renewed. To guard against this, the retailer must either buy of the wholesale dealer in whom he has perfect confidence, or else buy direct of the Importer. Mocha coffee, arriving in Boston direct by vessel, can always be found and bought in the original package in which it left Aden. Mocha is imported in 80 and 40 lb. packages. The inside covering is a specie of cocoa matting. Two of these packages termed quarters, or four termed eights, are enclosed in a coarse, strong covering of a material similar to palm leaves and pampas grass and tied with strong manilla rope, or with native woven rope. The consumptionof Mocha is increasing very rapidly, particularly in New England. It possesses such a peculiar flavor that it does not make a palatable drink alone, but no lover of a cup of coffee will forget its fragrance when combined with Java, or relinquish it when once its splendid qualities are known. The imports of Mocha received into the United States average about 15,000 bales annually, only about one half of which is probably of Arabian growth.

Ceylon coffee takes its name from the Island of Ceylon, where it grows and is to day the great rival of Java in the East. Colombo, is the port of shipment, and most of the Ceylon goes to England. It is divided into two classes, Plantation and Native. Plantation Ceylon takes high rank and is considered one of the finest coffees grown. It is raised on elevated lands, the greatest care being taken in its cultivation. It is a very solid, oily bean, transparent in color, and is largely consumed in Europe, where it is very highly prized, occupying the position there that Padang Java does in the United States. It is packed in small and large casks. Native or common Ceylon is raised on the low lands and resembles in color and size of bean Maracaibo or Savanilla, but lacks the strength of either. It is quite poor, drinks weak, and in coffee parlance, roasts quakery, resulting from the numerous blighted or undeveloped beans which possess little virtue or strength. Considerable quantities of Male-berry or Pea-berry Ceylon are shipped to this country and are used as a substitute for Male-berry Java.

Maracaibo coffee is a product of the northern part of South America, being raised in Venezuela. Like Java coffee, it is grown in different districts, each district producing a distinct variety, which are known as Cucuta, Merida, Tovar, Bocono and Trujillo. Maracaibo is the principal shipping port. The coffee is brought to this country in sailing vessels and steamers ; only light draft vessels can cross the dangerous bar at the entrance of the harbor, and in case of shipment by steamer, it has to be lightered over the bar. The trade is principally controlled by Spanish houses, who have almost a monopoly of it, and it is difficult for outside merchants to operate successfully in the goods there. This added to the fact that the country is often in a state of anarchy, make the receipts vary.

The crop of Maracaibo is quite large and the bulk of it is consumed in the United States, the receipts in 1880, amounting to about 12,000 tons. It is received here between the months of December and April, the lower grades arriving first, and finest grades not until March and April. Cucuta and Merida rank the highest, and justly so. The former grows on the lowlands and is a medium sized bean, light colored coffee. When first received here however, the color is green and it is usually kept in store, allowing it to thoroughly dry and bleach, when it assumes a yellowish hue, enhancing its market value one to two cents per lb.; the fancy marks of this coffee sometimes selling as high as Java. Merida or Mountain coffee as it is called, is grown

27

on high lands, and is a very hard grain heavy bean, dark color and never attains the light, yellowish shade of Cucuta. After roasting, it is impossible to distinguish it from Padang Java in style. It is heavier drinking than Cucuta, and possesses a more distinct acid flavor. Comparatively very little of these coffees go into consumption as Maracaibo. Probably no coffee raised is sold under such false colors as this. It has been found to be an excellent substitute for Java and also for mixing with Java, and its use for this purpose is fully recognized by the trade. The United States consume five times as much coffee under the name of Java as there is actually imported into the country, and we are forced to admit that the Cucuta and Merida varieties of Maracaibo coffee are the pack horses which carry most of the above load.

Tovar, Bocono and Trujillo grades differ essentially in point of quality from Cucuta and Merida. The bean is irregular in size, and owing to carelessness on the plantations in gathering, small stones are found mixed with it. The resemblance to Java is not sufficient to be used as a substitute or even for mixing with Java, but they are usually sold for what they are, Maracaibo coffee. They drink rank and possess a peculiar flavor. This is especially so of Trujillo, a large proportion of which resembles Rio in flavor. They sell from 2 to 4 cents less than Merida or Cucuta. Maracaibo coffees are packed in a peculiar bag, made of string, resembling a fine net, the contents being plainly seen through the meshes. They have distinguishing marks, denoting the districts where the contents were grown, viz : the finest grade of Cucuta is marked C. C., under the importers initials. The ordinary grades C. Merida M. Trujillo T, for best. T. T., denoting poorest.

Savanilla coffee is grown in the United States of Colombia, separated from the Cucuta district by a high range of mountains, over which the coffee has to be transported on the backs of mules to reach the shipping port of Maracaibo.

It is a light colored bean of the same general style and quality as the better grades of Maracaibo, but averaging larger in size and combining the united peculiarities of both Cucuta and Merida. After it leaves the hands of the Importers and Jobbers it is rarely known as Savanilla, but is rechristened Padang Java and is distributed through out the country as such. It arrives in the United States packed in cloth bags, which have no distinguishing marks.

Bogota and Coban coffee, other South American products are finding their way to the United States and are becoming favorably known. They roast Java style, being large and handsome beans and are used for the same general purposes as their cousins Maracaibo and Savanilla, namely, mixing with Java.

Jamaica coffee is grown on the Island of Jamaica and is much superior to any other variety grown on the West Indies; it possesses fine aromatic qualities, and is very popular with intelligent coffee dealers. That raised on the lowlands has in appearance all the characteristics of ordinary St. Domingo, but is of much finer flavor. It is usually shipped to market in large bags, varying in weight from 140 to 300 lbs. ; it was formerly put up very irregular, without sorting, the same bag often containing five or six different qualities. Traversing this island its entire length is a range of mountains on whose slopes and table lands is raised a coffee known as Blue Mountain Jamaica, which certainly possesses as much merit as any coffee raised, its solid, heavy, oily bean, almost transparent in color, will when roasted and ground make a delicious and fragrant cup of coffee. It is shipped largely to England, where its splendid qualities are appreciated. It is usually packed in barrels or casks, and with the exception of Plantation Ceylon is the only coffee so exported.

The more prominent coffees of Central America are Nicaragua, San Salvador, Guatamala and Costa Rica, all of which are at times sold as Costa Rica. This last coffee has a peculiar, positive flavor, is dark liquor in the cup, very strong and acid to the taste. In color the bean is green and generally semi-transparent, in size is often large and flat, and is highly prized by experts as an excellent coffee. It has many attributes of other coffees, especially that of Mocha, and there is no doubt but what selected Costa Rica will make a cup of coffee which would and does entitle it to take high rank. The fact that much of it is either hidey or sour, renders the purchase of it very risky, and only they who are acquainted with this peculiarity and are competent to detect it, can with any safety purchase or use it. It combines readily with other coffees, and for mixing is second to none. Nearly all of the coffee is shipped to San Francisco and is controlled by coffee importers on the Pacific side.

Guatamala coffee has many of the qualities of Costa Rica and is often sold as such. It is not so liable to be sour. It is picked with more care, often washed, cleansed and freed from all impurities, in fact, no coffee comes to this market in so uniformly good condition. It drinks like a Costa Rica only smoother, lacking its pungency, roasts handsomely, and develops one peculiarity after roasting, the bean cracks open, showing the white hull, and is very attractive in style, either raw or roasted. It is universally coming into favor and its production promises to be doubled within the next five years. It is very largely used in the West and is sold and consumed on its merits.

San Salvador coffee is similar to Guatamala but not so handsome or stylish; it drinks well, and has, when brought to market and exposed to the air, a sweet smell resembling Chocolate or Cocoa, and is inclined to turn light yellow or straw color with age.

Nicaragua coffee is among the poorest of the Central American products; it is not particularly stylish, and in color is of a dull grey hue or mottled straw and has only fair drinking qualities.

Laguayra coffee is raised in Venezuela, a South American State. This coffee is of a dark green color and small bear, similar in appearance to Rio, and when Rio has been scarce it has been polished and sold as such. It possesses mild qualities, but often develops more or less Rio flavor; much of it is used in Pennsylvania and the West, and some goes into consumption in New England.

Cape Haytien, St. Marc and St. Domingo coffees are grown on the island of Hayti or San Domingo. They do not rank very high, are large kernels, broad and flat, and often pressed out of shape in process of curing. These coffees are not in much favor in the United States, owing partially to the imperfect mode of picking, curing, &c.

Cape Haytien and St. Marc productions have a slight preference in market value over San Domingo coffee. Since the abolition of slavery there has been a falling off of the production, as the natives, left to their own inclination, where nature furnishes all they desire in the way of eatables (which grow spontaneously), sun themselves without thought or care. It is brought to this country in vessels loaded partially with logwood, but most of it is re-exported to the countries bordering on the Mediterranean Sea. It drinks fairly well, but is not much used for mixing; it sells for about three quarters of the price of good Maracaibo.

Mexican Coffee. The improvement in this variety has been something wonderful. Five years ago the demand was very limited, owing to its particularly poor drinking qualities, but at the present time this peculiarity has nearly disappeared, and some exceedingly fine coffees are being received from Mexico, ranking equal to any of the South American mild grades, the rancid, disagreeable flavor once disgustingly noticeable, having entirely disappeared. The two principal producing districts are Cordova and Oajaca. The Cordova product is a large sized, light colored bean, resembling fine Maracaibo, in appearance green, roasting large and smooth, and possesses a peculiar flavor in the cup, somewhat resembling Mocha. That grown in the Oajaca district resembles Plantation Ceylon in style of roast and drinking qualities. But comparatively few of the wholesale dealers have as yet awoke from their Rip Van Winkle sleep, enough to realize that growing almost in their back yard is a coffee, which, when roasted and served on the breakfast table makes a cup of coffee surpassed but by few. And it is fortunate in one sense that it is so, as the supply at present is so limited that it is sold almost immediately on arrival, the price realized being about the same as for better grades of Maracaibo. Mexico has great future capabilities and when the government becomes safe and free from anarchy, and the railroads which the government are subsidizing, have been extended throughout the coffee districts, it is more than probable that it will rival the present great producing countries, especially South America and the East Indies. Porto Rico at one time produced a coffee of that name, which was exceedingly popular, and the sale in this country, both east and west was large, but like Costa Rica coffee, it is inclined to become sour and hidey, and the experience of the trade has been such as to entirely stop the demand. It resemble Costa Rica in style of bean and have about the same market value.

Liberia produces a variety of coffee but little used, and in our opinion the public appreciating a fine cup of coffee are none the losers. It has very marked peculiarities. It is a large misshapen bean and drinks strong and rank, possessing no fine qualities. With the exception of Mocha its market value is the highest of any on the list, owing no doubt to its scarcity and the demand for it as a novelty.

African coffee grown on the east coast of Africa is a small sized bean, gnarley and unsightly in appearance, resembling Liberian. In the cup it drinks rank, harsh flavored and generally disagreeable and is very unsalable

Manilla coffee is the product of the Island of Manilla and is only occasionally imported into this country. It possesses no qualities that would recommend it, drinking like many of the package preparations labelled coffee.

Malabar coffee is a product of the East India Islands and is a fine variety. The bulk of the crop is shipped to Alexandria, where it is repacked and sold as Mocha.

California has turned her attention to the growth of coffee, but as yet it has not passed beyond the limits of experiment. The samples that have been received, show a large white bean with flavor resembling Costa Rica, from which seed it is raised.

We have now arrived at the end of the list which comprises all of the commercially known coffees of the world. Additional details could be written, but they would be of no practical advantage to the Retail Grocer, for whose benefit this pamphlet was written. You may be interested to know that the distinctive flavors, noticeable in the different varieties mentioned are attributed entirely to the peculiarities of the soil and climate where they flourish, as recent experiments have clearly shown that East India trees producing mild coffees, will, when transplanted to Brazil, furnish a coffee which develops strong Rio characteristics, and to all intents and purposes a Rio coffee. Careful cultivation and curing improves the market value, but it rests with soil and climate to stamp its distinctive flavor.

TARES ON COFFEE.

KIND.	Style of Package.	Per Ct.	Lbs.
Java	Pockets	1	. . .
"	Bags	2	. . .
Mocha	(Covers)	Actual	. . .
"	½ Bales	. . .	6
"	¼ Bales	. . .	4½
"	⅛ Bales	. . .	3
Rio	Bags	1	. . .
Santos	Bags	1	. . .
Jamaica	Bags	. 2	. . .
"	Barrels	Actual	. . .
Cape	Bags	2	. . .
Maracaibo	Bags	1	. . .
Savanilla	Bags	1	. . .
Ceylon	Bags	2	. . .
"	Barrels	Actual	. . .
Laguayra	Bags	Actual	. . .
Costa Rica	Bags	1	. . .
Angostura	Bags	Actual	. . .

TABLE OF STATISTICS

Showing where the United States received its supply in year 1880, and amount from each.

Those marked with an * are non-producing countries.

Brazil,	296,731,718	lbs.
Venezuela,	35,518,910	"
Dutch East Indies,	28,033,008	"
Central America,	19,254,218	"
Hayti,	22,659,285	"
Mexico,	9,818,525	"
U. S. of Colombia,	12,687,423	"
British West Indies and Honduras,	2,049,577	"
*England,	5,517,103	"
British East Indies,	4,647,062	"
China, Hong Kong, and other Asiatic Countries,	1,043,535	"
*Netherlands,	3,083,840	"
Hawaiian Islands,	77,923	"
Liberia,	143,781	"
Porto Rico,	2,937,083	"
Dutch West Indies and Dutch Guiana,	1,204,363	"
British Possessions in Africa and adjacent Islands,	594,051	"
Africa,	1,220	"
Spanish possessions and others,	9,733	"
Danish West Indies,	239,902	"
Peru,	840	"
French possessions in Africa and adjacent Islands,	1,442	"
*Germany,	238,495	"
Cuba,	29,538	"
*Belgium,	79,492	"
Azores, Maderia, Cape de Verde Islands,	1,286	"
Turkey in Africa,	10,300	"
British Guiana,	170	"
*Provinces of Quebec, Ontario, Manitoba, etc.,	329	"
France and French West Indies,	33,905	"
*Portugal and Spain,	1,870	"
San Domingo,	150,709	"

TOTAL, . . 446,850,727 lbs.

VALUE, . . $60,360,769

35

SKIMMINGS.

THE City of New York is commencing to command attention as a coffee producing district, contributing what is known on the market as skimmings. This variety is literally what its name indicates, and the process of obtaining it is as follows :—A greater or less portion of each cargo is found on arrival to have become damaged on the voyage by dampness, discoloring the bean and rendering it musty and mouldy. That portion of the cargo packed along the sides and top of the hold are more or less stained, and can be easily detected by the outward appearance of the bag or mat. These are cut open and the damaged beans are skimmed off; the remainder are then rebagged and sold as sound coffee, although it is an open question whether they can be considered as such. Many good judges maintain that as coffee is very susceptible to outside flavors, the odor of the mouldy beans penetrate through the whole bag. The skimmings of Java after being rebagged are classified and marked by a small stencil or brush on one corner of the package, as follows : G. S. signifying good skimmings ; P. S. poor skimmings ; S. S. store sweepings. In appearance good Java skimmings show very little damage, in fact, unless closely examined, would pass for a sound coffee and sell readily for from 2 to 3 cents per lb. less than the straight goods, in fact the demand is in excess of the supply, and this is met by using Singapore Java, (which we have described as very offensive in the cup), and coloring by sweating, South American mild coffees, taking care to sprinkle in a few damaged or black beans, in order to fully stamp them as skimmings. After roasting, it is impossible to detect these goods from sound coffee by their appearance. But it is very rare to find a lot that in the cup does not develop musty flavors, the fine delicate qualities of the coffee being entirely killed. The majority of the wholesale dealers buy their coffee on its style, color and general appearance, without roasting a small sample lot and testing its drinking qualities. You can readily perceive the result by following such a method.

Rios are classified in the same way only with an additional letter denoting the color of the goods, viz: G. L. S. signifying good light skimmings, and G. D. S. signifying good dark skimmings. Owing to the short time occupied on the passage, Rio as compared with Java varieties arrive in much better condition, and to all intents and purposes Rio skimmings are equal to sound Rio, in fact they often bring a higher price on the market, as some dealers believe they roast better and drink stronger on account of the added moisture, and their flavor in the cup is not affected.

Ground stain is another feature of damage caused by imperfect methods of curing. In some localities the green coffee is spread on the ground to dry, this becomes impregnated with sand and dust, and no amount of roasting will eradicate it. The result is an unsalable coffee in appearance although not affecting its drinking qualities.

Roasting and Grinding.

E will take it for granted that there is not a retail grocer in New England but what will acknowledge that the present system of roasting coffee by machinery, controlled by skillful workmen, offers superior advantages over the old methods, whether it be the primitive family skillet or the small portable machines turned by hand, which some retailers use. If there are any in doubt we would respectfully ask them to compare a sample from some large wholesale coffee house, with the product of their individual efforts and note the difference. Bear in mind this fact, and it is a settled fact that the most important conditions necessary to the securing of a cup of good coffee is the roasting of the bean properly, as the slightest variation from what is established as the correct roast will completely change the character of the drink. Perhaps a description of the methods employed by the leading coffee dealers will be found interesting.

The machine consists of a large round cylinder, revolving regularly and moved by steam power, suspended over a coal fire. The entire surface of the cylinder being perforated with small holes allows the heat to penetrate evenly and thoroughly. At one end is a hopper into which the green coffee is poured, and through the centre is a long tryer enabling the operator to ascertain just how far the roast has advanced. As soon as the coffee is sufficiently browned it is emptied into a large square box with a wire screen bottom, termed a cooler, the operator in the meantime throws over the hot coffee a small quantity of cold water. The rapid vaporizing of the water carries off the heat, and the changes wrought during this part of the process cause the berry to swell, thus giving it a much more sightly and attractive appearance. The addition of water does not, as might be supposed, add to the weight of the coffee, for the heat is so intense as to immediately convert the water into steam which readily escapes. At an opening in the end of the cooler is fitted a powerful blower, forcing cold air through the heated beans until they assume a condition which allows of their being handled. Meanwhile the coffee is thoroughly agitated while cooling as the oil of the coffee would appear on the surface if allowed to remain quiet. The ordinary size of machines used have a holding capacity of 300 lbs., although 200 lbs. is the amount usually roasted at one time. Forty-five minutes is the average time consumed for each roast, but the entire process of roasting, cooling and emptying occupies about an hour. Roasted coffee should be packed and kept in airtight packages as the aroma is constantly escaping from the time it leaves the roaster and is continually absorbing moisture which destroys its life and fragrance. Pine boxes or bins should never be used, as roasted coffee readily absorbs the wood flavor, which can easily be detected in the drink. Some of the more enterprising coffee dealers now ship roasted goods in tin cans hermetically sealed, with a holding capacity of 25 and 50 lbs. each, and we believe the time is not far distant before retail grocers will demand this style of package.

The shrinkage of coffee by roasting averages 15 to 16 per cent. ; extremely green lots loosing 18 per cent., while a very old coffee will not loose over 12 or 13 per cent. The roasting process will develop in every coffee more or less of what is termed in coffee parlance, quakers. Too much importance is attached to these kernels, many supposing that their presence indicates a mixture. Such is not the case, they are simply a bean, which while on the trees become sun-dried, the oil or caffeine, which is the essence of coffee, evaporating, leaving nothing but a lifeless berry; they roast white, and are perfectly tasteless. Our idea of a correct roast is to give the coffee a light chestnut-brown color, although the trade in different sections of New England differ in their opinions, some preferring a dark mahogany color. Our experience leads us to believe that the fine essential qualities necessary to securing a good cup of coffee are killed by over-roasting, in order to produce this color, and we would not recommend it.

Simple as it may seem, the process of grinding the roasted bean is one that requires more attention than what is at present given to it. Coarse ground coffee requires protracted boiling to extract its strength, and much boiling is fatal to a good cup of coffee. While one may grind too finely, the mistake of grinding too coarsely, is that most frequently made. Just to what degree of fineness it should be ground depends somewhat on the manner of making the coffee. There are three distinct methods employed in making coffee, as follows:—boiling, leaching or filtering, and by infusion. The first method by boiling is the most common one, and the coffee used should be ground so that the larger particles would not exceed in size, the head of a pin, while for the other two methods, the coffee should be ground very fine, and we believe it is of the utmost importance to the retail grocer that he should discover just what method each consumer uses, and adjust his mill to individual requirements.

MANIPULATION & ADULTERATION.

HE manipulation of coffee is so wide spread that to enter into all the details would consume more time than we can spare to write, or the reader to peruse, and think it will suffice to give a hurried description of the most important processes. Probably no one article in the world is subject to so successful manipulation as coffee. It commences from the time the berry is picked and prepared for the market, and continues until it reaches the consumer.

The producer mixes the leavings and tail ends of the old crop with the new, when he can successfully. The middle men or commission agents at the principal points where coffee is accumulated for shipment, manipulate it by changing packages and marks, polish it or paint it (for coloring done by chemicals amounts to the same thing), and so alter the marks, color and appearance, as to make it sell more readily. On its arrival in this country the coffee is turned out of its original packages, shovelled over, marks again changed, and bags turned inside out, sweated or colored artificially, as the trade desire or the necessity of the removing the traces of damage require.

Java skimmings are picked over by children, the black beans eliminated, the balance rematted and sold as sound, but as before stated, the taint remains, which no amount of labor or human ingenuity can remove. An average of 1,000 mats monthly of this coffee has been bought by wholesale dealers in Boston, and by them distributed throughout New England to the retailers as sound first class goods.

All varieties of coffee pass through more or less manipulation, but not always to the injury of the goods or detremental to the buyer.

Rio coffee is polished by machinery, and colored in different shades. The golden hue is applied by the use of tumeric ; light slate color, by the use of soap-stone. This does not affect its drinking qualities, but simply enhances its commercial value in appearance. Maracaibo and other mild coffees are made more salable by resorting to a process known as milling, which consists of running the coffee through brushes, removing all dust and dirt from the bean, giving it a uniform color and appearance.

Under the head of adulteration little can be said. Owing to the present cheapness of pure coffee, the system of combining foreign substances with it is a thing of the past.

More or less cheap mixtures are sold in package form ; but it is universally understood that they are mixtures consisting of chicory, peas, rye, &c., and contain but a limited per centage of coffee.

Every coffee mill in a retail grocer's store, is a nail in the coffin of adulterated coffees, as by purchasing the whole roasted bean, and grinding it themselves, you obtain nothing but pure coffee of some grade.

General Remarks.

F ROM a total of yearly production of about 525,000 tons the United States consume an average of 156,482 tons ; this shows a rapid increase, as up to the year 1861, the average yearly consumption amounted to only about 79,848 tons. But bear in mind that marching side by side with increased consumption, and keeping pace with it is an improved public taste imperatively demanding finer drinking coffee.

Fifteen years ago the average quality of the coffee drank would not be tolerated in a county poor-house of the present day. Of all the table articles offered for sale by the retailer we know of none which adds to or detracts from his reputation so much as the quality of his coffee. We believe the retailers thoroughly realize this fact, and have striven long and honestly, making price a secondary consideration to secure a coffee that would perfectly satisfy the consumers. Those of you who have failed to do so may have been and are now at a loss to account for it. In our description of the varieties of coffees and the manipulations of the same, we have stated nothing but plain unvarnished truths which we are in a position to maintain. Should you reperuse the same you may be inclined to investigate your source of supply, and there find good cause for your non-success.

There are two distinct methods employed in the purchase of coffees by wholesale dealers at the present day.

One is (and it numbers among its followers by far the larger majority of buyers), to make the general appearance of the green berry such as color, size, and the district where it was supposed to have been produced, the only standard for determining its quality and adaptability to satisfy the wants of customers. We unhesitatingly pronounce this method to be directly responsible for the failure of so many retailers to obtain even running fine coffee. We will not consider the liability they incur to have artificially colored or damaged goods foisted upon them, but take it for granted that in each and every case they are fortunate enough to secure straight Jave coffee. (We use the term Java in our argument for the reason that the trouble invariably occurs in that variety.) The result is not changed for the reason that two coffees of equal commercial value, in appearance green, arriving on the same ship are liable to be wide apart in cup value, one developing full rich qualities, the other the reverse. Do you suppose for one instant that you can obtain even running pure coffee from such a source? As well might you be ieve that a cup of pure water can be obtained from a brook whose fountain head starts in a barn-yard.

The other method of purchasing is to roast by hand a small sample of the coffee under consideration—grinding, weighing carefully in fine adjusted scales, and placing on the sample table by the side of some coffee which has given complete satisfaction and stamped its reputation. Color and appearance green is completely ignored, and in their place drinking qualities receive paramount attention. This process is pursued by comparatively few, as it takes years of careful application and general adaptability to succeed as a coffee expert. It requires something more than honesty and good intentions to do a jobbing coffee business at the present day, although they are necessary requisites; in addition, must be a complete knowledge of the facts in regard to adulterations and ability to detect the same. We strongly advise the retailers who are de-sirous of securing the finest and most uniform coffee to place their orders with houses who make a specialty of this article, as the time, care and knowledge necessary to secure successful results cannot be given by dealers who make coffee one of many articles they purchase and sell. This rule applies to mercantile business with equal force as to professional callings. For a scientific treatment of the eye would you go to the family physician or to the Oculist?

After you have purchased your roasted coffee don't put it in a wooden bin or box, or leave it exposed to the air, it will certainly absorb moisture which deadens it and the woody flavor will be noticeable in the drink. " Keep your coffee in a tin can."

See that your coffee mill grinds evenly—an old style of mill will not. The improved mills are the best, and can be adjusted to the requirements of each customer. You will be repaid for your trouble by the increased satisfaction it will give.

SPECIAL.

WE stated in our introductory that this pamphlet was written with the object to present facts and information which could be utilized by the retail grocers of New England. It was not intended as an advertising medium, but now that the story of coffee is told, we feel we have the right to call attention briefly to our facilities for transacting a wholesale tea and coffee business. We are, strictly speaking, a specialty house, dealing in teas and coffees exclusively. Our store, located at 87 Broad (front entrance), 8 Hamilton Street (rear entrance), is a building 110 feet long and 7 stories high (see cut in front of book). In the basement, which is free from dampness, we store our green coffee. On the first floor can be found our counting rooms, tea sampling office and salesroom, also floor room for the storage of teas. The second floor is used for the storage of teas, and in the front part are our private offices and coffee testing and sampling room. Storage of teas and coffee occupies the third and fourth floors. On the fifth can be found our roasting, sifting and grinding machines, combining all the latest improvements. The fifth and sixth floor we devote to the manufacture and storing of tin cans, in which we ship the most of our coffee. We have no spare room, it all being needed and utilized, and we cordially invite the trade to inspect our establishment at any time they may find it convenient. We have no carefully guarded secrets, either in our stock of coffee or manufacture of the same, and you will always find free access to our entire building.

We import our teas, and also buy in large invoices, and we can and will make it for your advantage to consult us when purchasing.

In our coffee department can be found every variety of coffee grown, which the general trade require, provided they possess intrinsic merit in the cup. All others are discarded. Damaged or artificially colored coffee of whatever commercial value we carefully avoid, knowing that the handling of these goods must result in a serious loss of trade.

In our roasting establishement we recognize that it requires skill, and secure such workmen, knowing that upon the roast depends largely the success of the coffee. We roast only to supply the demands of our own business, therefore, we do not keep roasted coffee in stock, but each and every order is filled from the roasting of the day on which it is received, insuring crisp, fresh coffee, on arrival at the retailer's store. Another safeguard used by us is to test each roast separately, which does away with all possible chance for a mistake.

Previous to three years ago, we sold as good, but no better coffee than our many competitors. This position afforded us neither a special reputation or increased patronage, and we were not satisfied to stop at that point, but commenced investigating the merits of different high grade Javas, among others, the products of the private plantations of the Island of Java. This resulted in placing upon the market our "Standard" Java. Here we date the commencement of the improvement in our coffee business, and from an average monthly sale of 20,000 lbs., we have steadily increased, until our sales for the month of December, 1881, amounted to 100,177 lbs., or a trifle over 50 tons of roasted coffees. That it is the finest and most uniform

Java coffee on the market, over 1,500 retail grocers in New England, who are now using it, can testify.

We respectfully submit the following testimonial, calling your particular attention to the high reputation enjoyed by the endorsers : —

Boston, January 2, 1882.

Messrs. Chase & Sanborn, Boston.

Dear Sirs:—In preparing our CONDENSED COFFEE (which is pure extract of coffee, sugar and cream combined, ready for use) we use none but the best materials obtainable, and during the past twenty years we have tried all the high grades of coffee found in this market, for the purpose of ascertaining that which contained the *greatest strength* and *finest flavor*.

We are now using your "STANDARD JAVA" exclusively, because we have found, by actual test, that it uniformly possesses *greater strength* and *finer flavor* than any coffee we have ever used.   Respectfully,

[Signed]   W. K Lewis & Brothers,
                          93 and 95 Broad Street, Boston.

Our firm consists of the following members : —

CALEB CHASE,   JAS. S. SANBORN,   CHAS. D. SIAS

ably supported by thirteen salesmen, as follows : —

I. E. BROWN,	WM. D. RAND,
I. H. BROWN,	JOHN MORIARTY, ·
NOYES AMES,	I. H. AMES,
PATRICK H. FARREN,	JOSEPH PERRY,
G. T. BASSETT,	D. F. SANBORN,
CHAS. E. SANBORN,	WILLIAM RICE,

HORACE E. GOULD.

We think we can feel justly proud of the above support, comprising as they do, gentlemen who by years of honest, careful, intelligent attention to the wants of customers, have established a large personal following.   Most of them have been associated with us for years, the others having attracted our attention by sharp, vigorous competition.   We have only been too glad to avail ourselves of their assistance.

Feeling that they do not need any recommendation from us.   We remain, very truly yours,

                          CHASE & SANBORN.

A great many testimonials have no weight in the minds of the reader, from the fact that their origin is in some distant location, which completely prevents the establishing of their genuineness. In presenting the following, we do so with the sincere hope they may be read carefully, as they deserve to be, for they are written by representative grocers, in fact your own neighbors, whose integrity cannot be questioned, or whose opinions bought.

TESTIMONIALS.

NEWBURYPORT, MASS., Dec. 16th, 1881.

Messrs. CHASE & SANBORN.

Gentlemen:—You are welcome to use our name as testifying to the fact that your Standard Java suits complete. No trouble, but always right.

Yours truly,

J. J. & W. WOODS.

PORTSMOUTH, N. H., Dec. 27th, 1881.

Messrs. CHASE & SANBORN:

We have sold your Standard Java for two years and hope that the quality of the past will be maintained in the future. It could not be better, and gives perfect satisfaction.

Respectfully yours,

J. H. WELLS & SON.

PORTSMOUTH, N. H., Nov. 24th, 1881.

Messrs. CHASE & SANBORN.

Gentlemen:—By using your Standard Java Coffee I have not only suited my customers but have increased my coffee trade. Shall be pleased to give you my orders in the future, as I want the Standard Java.

Yours truly,

H. C. RUSSELL.

Messrs. CHASE & SANBORN.   KITTERY, ME., Dec. 1881.

Gentlemen :—We believe it is to our advantage to sell your Standard Java Coffee exclusively. Our customers speak highly of it and our own taste allows us to make the statement that we consider it the best coffee for us to buy.

                    Yours truly,
                                        LEWIS & BROOKS.

Messrs. CHASE & SANBORN.   CANTON, N. Y., Dec. 30th, 1881.

Gentlemen :—Having been a customer of yours in the purchase of your Standard Java Coffee for the last year, it is with pleasure that I can safely say that I have never had a coffee that has given as good satisfaction as the Standard. I have kept it con_ stantly on hand for one year and have built up a very satisfactory trade upon its merits.

                    Very truly, &c., &c
                                        H. A. POSTE.

Messrs. CHASE & SANBORN.   BOSTON, Jan. 2d, 1882.

Gentlemen :—We have been selling your "Standard" Java Coffee in our five stores in Maine, for a number of months past and it has given universal satisfaction. While we have it, we have no fear that our customers will say "can get better coffee at the other stores," for the reason that your "*Standard*" *Java is the best*. Keep it up to its present high standard and you will merit and undoubtedly secure for it the success wished for you by

                    Yours very truly,
                                        F. SHAW & BROTHERS.
[Signed.]   Per J. B. CHAPIN, JR.,
                                             Purchasing Agent.

Messrs. CHASE & SANBORN :   BOSTON, Jan. 3d, 1882.

We were persuaded fifteen months ago to try a sample lot of your "Standard" Java. We are perfectly satisfied with it for the simple reason that our customers without exception pronounce it a fine drinking coffee. We believe it has *contributed largely* to our reputation and success as dealers in fine groceries.

                    SMITH & WARD, No. 123 Lincoln St., Boston.

Messrs. CHASE & SANBORN.   BOSTON, January 17th, 1881.

Gentlemen :—Having used your Standard Coffee for the past two years, we are pleased to state that it has given better satisfaction than any other we ever used, always being uniform and never varying in excellence. Our patrons demand the choicest of articles and we believe that your Standard Java has built up our reputation as fancy grocers as much as any other article in our store.

                    Very Resp. Yours,
                                        BAKER & CUTLER, 216 Clarendon St.

Messrs. CHASE & SANBORN.
HOLYOKE. MA-- January 20th, 1882.

Gentlemen :—You are at liberty to use my name as recommending your Standard Java. I have used it for a year past, occasionally buying other coffees, which were highly praised by the owner, but they do not suit my trade as your Standard does. I believe it has certainly increased my coffee trade and I know it gives perfect satisfaction

Yours truly,

JOHN DOYLE.

Messrs. CHASE & SANBORN.
MIDDLEBURY, VT., January 6th, 1882.

Gentlemen :—The Coffee purchased of your house has given perfect satisfaction, and our coffee sales have increased the past year.

Yours, &c.,

BECKWITH & CO.

Messrs. CHASE & SANBORN, 87 Broad St., Boston.
CONCORD, N. H. Sept. 16th, 1881.

Dear Sirs :—Your "Standard" Java Coffee is giving the best satisfaction of any we have ever sold in our experience of fourteen years. Please send a barrel next week, as usual.

Yours truly,

E. D. CLOUGH & CO.

Messrs. CHASE & SANBORN.
WORCESTER, MASS. Dec. 30th, 1881.

Gentlemen :—Please send me at your earliest convenience one Bbl. of "Roasted Standard Java." I feel like saying a good word in regard to above goods, for since I commenced using the "Standard" I have had a constantly increasing Coffee trade, and it is to the uniform excellence of your goods I owe the same. Wishing you the compliments of the season I remain

Yours very truly,

GEO. A. PEARSON, Agent for Worcester Co-operative Association.

Messrs. CHASE & SANBORN.
NORTHFIELD, VT., Dec. 28th, 1881.

Gentlemen :—Yours of the 27th received, and in reply would say. I have sold your Standard Java Coffee for the past year and it has given entire satisfaction to my trade and would cheerfully recommend it to all who wish a fine pure coffee.

Yours truly,

A. E. DENNY.

Messrs. CHASE & SANBORN.
PORTLAND, ME., Dec. 22d, 1881.

Gentlemen :—We have sold your Standard Java Coffee for the past three years and it is certainly the best Java we can find. It gives perfect satisfaction to all our customers.

Very truly yours,

STEVENS & ELWELL.

TURNERS FALLS, MASS., Dec. 29th, 1881.

Messrs. CHASE & SANBORN.

Gentlemen :—We have used your Standard Java Coffee the past two years, and it is the best and gives the most satisfaction of any kind we ever sold.

Yours,

WISE & RIPLEY.

PORTLAND, ME., Dec. 30th, 1881.

Messrs. CHASE & SANBORN.

Gentlemen :—My coffee trade is yours so long as you keep the quality of your Standard Java up to what it has been for the last four years. I have used no other during that time, although I have been urged to change. But knowing that when I took hold of it my trade increased, and it gives perfect satisfaction, I think it my best policy to stick.

Yours truly,

GEO. A. GUPTILL & Co

HOLYOKE MASS., Nov. 26th, 1881.

Messrs. CHASE & SANBORN.

Gentlemen :—I have no complaints from your Standard Java, and after trying various kinds I am satisfied, for my finest Java, it is for my interests to use yours exclusively.

Yours very truly,

E. A. FENNO & CO.

TAUNTON, MASS., Nov. 20th, 1881.

Messrs. CHASE & SANBORN.

Gentlemen :—We have been selling Chase & Sanborn's "Standard" Java Coffee almost exclusively for two years, and our coffee trade has more than trebled during that time. We have no trouble in getting the same quality every time we order.

Very truly yours,

P. WILLIAMS & CO.

BOSTON, Dec. 12th, 1881.

Messrs. CHASE & SANBORN.

Gentlemen :—During the last year I have bought several different kinds of coffee, and from careful comparison I think your Standard Java is the best I have seen and shall use it exclusively for my best coffee.

Yours truly,

P. HIGGINS & Co., Cor. Essex St. & Harrison Ave.

DOVER, N. H., Dec. 25th, 1881.

Messrs. CHASE & SANBORN.

Gentlemen :—It gives me pleasure to state that your Standard Java seems to suit my trade and customers perfectly. I want no other so long as this is up to standard.

Yours truly,

P. McMANUS

BOSTON, MASS., Dec. 7th, 1881.

Messrs. CHASE & SANBORN.

Gentlemen:—Your Standard Java Coffee is giving the best satisfaction to our customers, and our coffee trade is steadily increasing.

Yours truly,

FISH & KEENE, 96 Blackstone St.

—

WHITE RIVER JUNCTION, VT., Dec. 28th, 1881.

Messrs. CHASE & SANBORN.

Gentlemen:—We have been using your Standard Java Coffee in the Junction House for several months past. It gives good satisfaction in strength and flavor. We have found none superior to it.

Yours truly,

C. B. BALLARD, Proprietor.

WORCESTER, MASS., Dec. 19th, 1881.

Messrs. CHASE & SANBORN.

Gentlemen:—Please send me by Worcester Dispatch, one Bbl. of Standard Java (bulk), and one box Standard Java (pkges.)

You will notice by the frequency of our orders that the demand for the Standard of us, is constantly increasing. Only keep the quality of the "Standard," up to the standard and a standard it shall remain, with

Yours respectfully,

E. B. PRINCE.

No. TROY, VT., January 4th, 1881.

Messrs. CHASE & SANBORN, Boston.

Gentlemen:—I have sold your "Standard" Java Coffee for the last two years, it has given general satisfaction to my customers.

I consider it the *best* coffee in the market.

Respectfully,

GEO. .P HARDY.

BOSTON, January 5th, 1882.

Messrs. CHASE & SANBORN.

We have been using your Coffee for the past two years, during which time we have probably drawn it by the side of fifty different coffees and as yet have been unable to match it. It has always given our trade perfect satisfaction.

Respectfully yours,

A. FELLOWS & CO., Cor. Washington and Concord Sts.

———

LEWISTON, ME., Nov. 16th, 1880.

Messrs. CHASE & SANBORN.

Gentlemen:—Please send us one barrel roasted "Standard" Java Coffee, same quality as last. We wish to say that it gives universal satisfaction and is by far the best coffee we have ever sold.

Respectfully yours,

DAY, NEALY & CO.

Messrs. CHASE & SANBORN.
WORCESTER, MASS., Nov. 20th, 1881.

Gentlemen :—Our customers are pleased with Chase & Sanborn's Standard Java Coffee.

J. E. HOOKER & Co.

Messrs. CHASE & SANBORN.
BOSTON, MASS., Nov. 18th, 1881.

Gentlemen :—Having bought and sold Chase & Sanborn's Standard Java Coffee, I can truly say it has proved to be the best coffe I have ever sold in twenty-six years' experience as a Wholesale Grocer.

HENRY S. BROWN, 19 & 20 India St.

Messrs. CHASE & SANBORN.
WATERBURY, VT., Dec. 29th, 1881.

Gentlemen :—Having used in my family and sold in my store your Standard Java Coffee, I can highly recommend it to be a tip top article, which gives universal satisfaction.

Very truly yours,

W. H. ASHLEY.

Messrs. CHASE & SANBORN.
BRIDGEPORT, CT., Dec. 29th, 1881.

In answer to your inquiry regarding your Standard Java Coffee would say : We have handled it for the past two years and it affords us pleasure to state, has given entire satisfaction. Not only does it draw trade, but holds it. We believe it to be *standard* in every sense of the word.

Very respectfully yours,

COBB & PERKINS.

Messrs. CHASE & SANBORN.
WORCESTER, MASS., Dec. 20th, 1881.

Gentlemen :—The coffee with which you have supplied us the past three years has given the most perfect satisfaction ; we find it always uniform and reliable.

We give it the preference to any kind we have tried. Success to the "Standard Java."

Yours truly,

SWASEY & LOUGEE.

Messrs. CHASE & SANBORN.
ST. JOHNSBURY, VT., Dec. 28th, 1881.

Gentlemen :—Your "Standard Java Coffee" gives the best satisfaction of any we have ever sold.

Yours truly,

E. F. & F. N. BROWN.

Messrs. CHASE & SANBORN.
LANCASTER, N. H., Dec. 29th, 1881.

Gentlemen :—We have used several barrels of your "Standard Java Coffee." We find it is excellent in flavor and strength, uniform in quality and suits our trade better than any we have ever sold.

Very respectfully, yours,

R. P. KENT, SON & Co.

BANGOR, ME., Nov. 10th, 1881.

Messrs. CHASE & SANBORN.

Gentlemen:—The coffee we have been selling for the last two years (your Standard Java) has given extra satisfaction, and we believe it to be the best quality that we have ever sold.

Yours truly,

THOMPSON & KELLOGG.

QUINCY, MASS., Nov. 25th, 1881.

Messrs. Chase & SANBORN.

Gentlemen;—I have used the "Standard" Java Coffee for over two years, and can thankfully say that it pleases my trade the best of any coffee I have ever sold. And from a thorough trial in my own family, I feel confident in recommending it to any one wanting a rich, fragrant, even running Java Coffee.

Respectfully yours,

JOHN F. MERRILL, Proprietor Boston Branch Store.

PORTLAND, ME., Dec. 18th, 1881.

Messrs. CHASE & SANBORN.

Gentlemen:—I found it difficult and almost impossible to suit my customers until I commenced selling your "Standard" Java Coffee. Since then I have had no complaints and am satisfied it is the best coffee I can buy.

Yours truly,

GEO. H. LORD.

LEWISTON, ME., Dec. 3d, 1881.

Messrs. CHASE & SANBORN.

Gentlemen;—Your Standard Java Coffee gives perfect satisfaction, runs even, and I consider it the best coffee for one to buy.

Yours truly,

D. E. PARLIN, Proprietor Boston Branch Grocery.

PROVIDENCE, R. I., Dec. 16th, 1881.

Messrs. CHASE & SANBORN.

Gentlemen;—Please send me one barrel "Roasted Standard Java." It gives perfect satisfaction, and I hope you will continue to keep it up to its present standard, which certainly is very fine.

Yours very truly,

D. W. HYDE.

WORCESTER, MASS., Dec. 29th, 1881.

Messrs. CHASE & SANBORN.

Gentlemen;—We take pleasure in adding our testimony to that of many others in regard to your "Standard Java Coffee. ⌐ We have tried most everything in the line of pure Javas and our experience, is that there is nothing that can compare with it, and we want no other while it is kept up to its present state of perfection. Having used it for about two years we know whereof we affirm.

Respectfully,

CROSS & PENTECOST.

BOSTON & MAINE RAILROAD DINING-ROOMS, EXETER, N. H.
Messrs. CHASE & SANBORN.

Gentlemen;—We have been using your Roasted Standard Java Coffee for the past year, for the simple and only reason that we consider it the finest flavored and most even running coffee in the market.

Very truly yours,

C. C. & R. A. LITTLEFIELD.

ROCKLAND, ME., Dec. 15th, 1881.
Messrs. CHASE & SANBORN.

Gentlemen.—We have sold your Standard Java Coffee for the past three years, and pronounce it the most even running coffee, and one that gives better satisfaction to our trade than any we ever handled,

Yours very truly,

COBB, WIGHT & Co., Wholesale and Retail Grocers.

PORTLAND, ME., Dec. 14th, 1881.
Messrs. CHASE & SANBORN.

Gentlemen;—For three years I have used your Standard Java Coffee. My customers I know, appreciate a fine Coffee, and your Standard is perfect in every respect

Yours respectfully,

M. A DILLINGHAM.

PORTLAND, ME., Dec. 9th, 1880.
Messrs. CHASE & SANBORN.

Gentlemen;—I consider your "Standard" Java the best coffee to drink or sell I can find. Have sold it for two years, and during that time I have had no complaints

Yours truly,

J. C. OSGOOD,

LACONIA, N. H., Nov. 12th, 1881.
Messrs. CHASE & SANBORN.

Gentlemen;—Please send me a barrel of Roasted Standard Java Coffee, as usual. Be sure and send the same quality that I have been having, as it gives extra satisfaction, and I cheerfully say I think it the best coffee I have ever sold.

Very truly yours,

W. L. SWAIN.

AUBURN, ME., Nov. 6th, 1881.
Messrs. CHASE & SANBORN.

Gentlemen:—Your Standard Java Coffee roasted, we have sold the year past, and say it gives us the best satisfaction of any coffee we ever sold. It suits every time.

Yours truly,

STIMSON & LEARNED.

GREENFIELD, MASS., Dec. 29th, 1881.

Messrs. CHASE & SANBORN.

Gentlemen:—Your Standard Java Coffee, is giving the best of satisfaction. My customers say it is the best coffee they can find.

Yours truly,

CHARLES KEITH.

PORTSMOUTH, N. H., Dec. 22d, 1881.

Messrs. CHASE & SANBORN.

Gentlemen:—For our best coffee we shall continue to use your "Standard" Java, provided you keep it up to its present excellence. It pleases my trade.

Yours respectfully,

D. J. LYNCH.

BRISTOL, R. I., Jan 31st, 1882.

Messrs. CHASE & SANBORN, 87 Broad Street, Boston, Mass.

Gentlemen:—I think if every grocer would keep your Standard Java for sale there would be less room for complaint regarding poor coffees. I have received a good many compliments on the merits of your Standard Java. Keep it up to the *Standard* and you can always depend on my coffee trade, which is increasing all the time since I commenced to use it.

Very respectfully yours,

J. P. THOMPSON.

BRISTOL, R. I., Jan. 31st, 1882.

Messrs. CHASE & SANBORN, Boston, Mass.

Gentlemen:—It is with pleasure I endorse the merits of your *Standard Java.* After many years of experience I must acknowledge it to be the very best Java I have found. Shall continue to use your Standard so long as you keep it as good as you have for the last nine months.

Yours most respectfully,

A. M. NEWMAN.

BRISTOL, R. I., Jan. 31st, 1882.

Messrs. CHASE & SANBORN, Boston, Mass.

Gentlemen:—After trying very numerous sample lots of the best Javas I could find, I have come to the conclusion that your *Standard Java* leads them all, being a splendid drinker, uniform in quality and always *reliable*. I can safely say that my coffee trade has more than doubled since I commenced using your Standard Java some ten months ago. None other than Standard Java for me so long as you keep it up to the present high grade.

Very truly yours,

FREDERICK CARD.

ROCKLAND, ME., Dec. 10th, 1881.

Messrs. CHASE & SANBORN, 87 Broad Street, Boston.

Gentlemen:—I have sold your "Standard" Java for three years, and consider it the most even running, and as giving the best satisfaction to my trade, of any coffee I can buy.

Very respectfully yours,

J. P. INGRAHAM.

Will the gentlemen who have so kindly and cheerfully assisted us by the use of their names and testimony, please accept our heartfelt thanks, assuring them that we shall earnestly and honestly strive to maintain the present good feeling.

CONTENTS.

www.ingramcontent.com/pod-product-compliance
Lightning Source LLC
Chambersburg PA
CBHW021637270326
41931CB00008B/1056